ACME Fast Freight, Inc., Merchant Shippers Association, Inc., et al., Appellants, v. United States of America, Interstate Commerce Commission and Lifschultz Fast Freight U.S. Supreme Court Transcript of Record with Supporting Pleadings

DAVID AXELROD, U.S. Supreme Court, DAVID AXELROD

ACME Fast Freight, Inc., Merchant Shippers Association, Inc., et al., Appellants, v. United
States of America, Interstate Commerce Commission and Lifschultz Fast Freight
Jurisdictional Statement / DAVID AXELROD / 1949 / 338 / 338 U.S. 855 / 70 S.Ct. 104 / 94 L.Ed. 524 / 9-16-1949
ACME Fast Freight, Inc., Merchant Shippers Association, Inc., et al., Appellants, v. United States of America, Interstate Commerce
Commission and Lifschultz Fast Freight
Motion / U.S. Supreme Court / 1949 / 338 / 338 U.S. 855 / 70 S.Ct. 104 / 94 L.Ed. 524 / 9-16-1949
ACME Fast Freight, Inc., Merchant Shippers Association, Inc., et al., Appellants, v. United States of America, Interstate Commerce
Commission and Lifschultz Fast Freight
Motion / DAVID AXELROD / 1949 / 338 / 338 U.S. 855 / 70 S.Ct. 104 / 94 L.Ed. 524 / 9-16-1949

ACME Fast Freight, Inc., Merchant Shippers
Association, Inc., et al., Appellants, v. United States
of America, Interstate Commerce Commission and
Lifschultz Fast Freight U.S. Supreme Court
Transcript of Record with Supporting Pleadings

Table of Contents

SUPREME COURT OF THE UNITED STATES

OCTOBER TERM, 1949

No. 338

ACME FAST FREIGHT, INC., ET AL.,
Appellants,

vs.

THE UNITED STATES OF AMERICA, INTERSTATE COMMERCE COMMISSION, ET AL.

APPEAL FROM THE UNITED STATES DISTRICT COURT FOR THE NORTHERN DISTRICT OF ILLINOIS

STATEMENT AS TO JURISDICTION

DAVID AXELROD,
JAMES L. GIVAN,
Counsel for Appellants.

INDEX

SUBJECT INDEX

CASES CITED

OTHER AUTHORITIES CITED

—4310

IN THE UNITED STATES DISTRICT COURT FOR THE NORTHERN DISTRICT OF ILLINOIS EASTERN DIVISION

Civil Action No. 49C 409

ACME FAST FREIGHT, INC., 2 Lafayette Street, New York, New York,

MERCHANT SHIPPERS ASSOCIATION, INC., 1858 South Western Avenue, Chicago 8, Illinois,

NATIONAL CARLOADING CORPORATION, 19 Rector Street, New York 6, New York,

PACIFIC AND ATLANTIC SHIPPERS ASSOCIATION, INC., 356 North Halsted Street, Chicago, Illinois,

UNIVERSAL CARLOADING & DISTRIBUTING CO., INC., 40 Rector Street, New York 6, New York, *Plaintiffs,*

vs.

UNITED STATES OF AMERICA AND THE INTERSTATE COMMERCE COMMISSION, *Defendants,*

and

LIFSCHULTZ FAST FREIGHT, *Intervening Defendant*

STATEMENT AS TO JURISDICTION

In compliance with Rule 12 of the Rules of the Supreme Court of the United States, as amended, Plaintiffs-Appellants submit herewith their statement particularly disclosing the basis upon which the Supreme Court of the United States has jurisdiction on appeal to review the judgment and decree of the District Court entered in this cause on April 27, 1949. A Petition for Appeal was filed on June 24, 1949, and is presented to the District Court herewith.

The jurisdiction of the Supreme Court to review by direct appeal the decision in this cause is conferred by the Judicial Code as revised by the Act approved June 25, 1948, effective September 1, 1948, entitled 28 U. S. Code, Sections 1253 and 2101(b), consolidating and continuing the substance of prior provisions of law relating to direct appeals from decisions of three-judge courts in suits to set aside orders of the Interstate Commerce Commission. The following decisions, appeals in which were taken pursuant to such prior provisions thus codified, sustain the jurisdiction of the Supreme Court to review the judgment on direct appeal in these cases, *United States* v. *Capital Transit Company*, 325 U. S. 357; *United States* v. *Detroit and Cleveland Navigation Company*, 326 U. S. 236; *United States* v. *Pennsylvania Railroad Company*, 323 U. S. 612; *United States* v. *Pierce Auto Freight Lines*, 327 U. S. 515.

Statutory Provisions Involved

This cause arises under Sections 410(c) and 410(d) of Part IV of the Interstate Commerce Act, 49 U. S. C. 1010(c) and 1010(d), which define the conditions under which the Interstate Commerce Commission may issue a permit to engage in business as a freight forwarder subject to Part IV of the Interstate Commerce Act. These Sections provide as follows:

> "(c) The Commission shall issue a permit to any qualified applicant therefor, authorizing the whole or any part of the service covered by the application, if the Commission finds that the applicant is ready, able, and willing properly to perform the service proposed, and that the proposed service, to the extent authorized by the permit, is or will be consistent with the public

interest and the national transportation policy declared
in this Act; otherwise such application shall be denied.
No such permit shall be issued to any common carrier
subject to part I, II, or III of this Act; but no application made under this section by a corporation controlled
by, or under common control with, a common carrier
subject to part I, II or III of this Act, shall be denied
because of the relationship between such corporation
and such common carrier.

"(d) The Commission shall not deny authority to
engage in the whole or any part of the proposed service
covered by any application made under this section
solely on the ground that such service will be in competition with the service subject to this part performed
by any other freight forwarder or freight forwarders."

The Facts of the Case

By an application filed in the proper form with the Interstate Commerce Commission, Lifschultz Fast Freight, which
is a freight forwarder, requested a permit authorizing it
to extend its service between points in and north and east
of Maryland, Pennsylvania, Ohio, Indiana, Illinois and
Wisconsin, on the one hand, and those in Minnesota, North
Dakota, Texas, New Mexico, Arizona, Nevada and California on the other hand. At the time this application was
filed, Lifschultz already was engaged in business as a
freight forwarder between points in and north and east of
Maryland and Pennsylvania, on the one hand, and points
within an approximate radius of 100 miles of Chicago on the
other hand.[1] After full hearing, the Interstate Commerce
Commission granted this application in part, authorizing

---

[1] Points in Milwaukee, Waukesha, Jefferson, Dane, Iowa, Grant, Lafayette, Green, Rock, Walworth, Racine, and Kenosha Counties, Wisconsin; Lake County, Indiana, and in Illinois in and north of the counties of
Adams, Brown, Cass, Menard, Logan, DeWitt, Piatt, Champaign, and
Vermillion; and in Iowa along the west bank of the Mississippi River
from Dubuque to Keokuk, inclusive.

Lifschultz to extend its service between the territory named in Footnote 1, on the one hand, and points in the States of Minnesota, California and Texas on the other hand, which States represent 98 percent of the tonnage potential of the entire territory applied for. The report and order of the Interstate Commerce Commission is dated September 16, 1948, and is entitled *Lifschultz Fast Freight Extension— West and Midwest*, 265 I. C. C. 431.

Thereafter these appellants, plaintiffs below, instituted an action in the United States District Court for the Northern District of Illinois, Eastern Division, pursuant to Title 28, U. S. Code, Sections 1336 and 2321 through 2325, inclusive, to enjoin and set aside the order of the Interstate Commerce Commission. On April 27, 1949, the District Court issued a decree accompanied by Findings of Fact and Conclusions of Law denying the relief applied for and dismissing the action.

The record before the Interstate Commerce Commission, an authenticated copy of which was filed with the District Court, discloses the following essential facts:

(1) Lifschultz Fast Freight has successfully engaged in the business of freight forwarding for a number of years. Its operations have been profitable and many of its patrons regard its service as superior to that of other freight forwarders.

(2) Lifschultz Fast Freight has adequate financial resources.

(3) Representatives of fourteen shippers who have utilized the service of Lifschultz Fast Freight in the past testified that they would use the proposed new service if it is instituted, subject to the following qualifications: (a) to the extent that they exercise the right to designate the transportation agency to be employed, and (b) if the new service

compares favorably in speed with other forwarders' services presently available in this territory.

None of these shippers disclosed specifically the tonnage which they would ship via Lifschultz nor, except very generally, the points to or from which it would move.

(4) Lifschultz proposes to follow the normal pattern of forwarder operations in conducting the proposed new service. This will include the utilization of truck or rail carriers as may be appropriate; the establishment of facilities wherever need therefor appears; the use of stoppage in transit as authorized by railroad tariffs; and joint loading with other freight forwarders as authorized in Section 404(d) of the Interstate Commerce Act, 49 U. S. C. 1004(d).

(5) No arrangements have been completed by Lifschultz with respect to the establishment of terminals; to obtaining joint loading contracts with other freight forwarders; or in the designation of truck or rail routes to be utilized.

(6) Approximately 75% of the traffic which moves in freight forwarder service is definitely routed by the consignee, rather than by the consignor.

(7) Fifteen consignees residing in the state of Texas and one residing in the state of California testified in opposition to the granting of the authority requested on the two grounds (a) that the freight forwarder service which they presently receive is adequate and satisfactory and the institution of an additional service might injure or impair the service which they are presently receiving, and (b) that their past experience with some freight forwarders who were unable to operate efficiently had been unsatisfactory and that they opposed the institution of any new service until it was shown that such service would be operated efficiently.

(8) Due to the greater distances between cities in the western territory proposed to be served; to the relatively lower population density in the west than in the east; and to the rate structure of the underlying rail carriers which must be utilized; there are serious operating difficulties which must be overcome before an efficient forwarder service can be performed in this territory. To illustrate, unless a forwarder has a sufficient volume of business to make direct cars to a large number of points scattered geographically through the territory, he is confronted with the alternative of making cars to only a few points and trucking freight from such points to its ultimate destination. This, however, is costly and time consuming. The resulting service would be inferior to that of forwarders who do make direct cars. To some extent, this problem is alleviated by the privilege of stopping cars in transit for partial unloading. However, in Texas only one intermediate stop is permitted so that at most one car can serve only two destinations. While the stopping in transit privilege is more liberal on the Pacific coast, there the rail rate structure is such that separate cars must be made for different classes of freight. Thus, any one day's forwarding to California would require a minimum of two cars because of the impossibility of mixing differently rated freight.

The evidence shows that to give the barest minimum of service to the state of Texas, four cars would be required and to give the barest minimum of service simply to Los Angeles and San Francisco, California, a minimum of ten cars weekly would be required. This minimum volume, to these two states alone, represents approximately 25,000 tons per year of new traffic which Lifschultz must obtain. This is an increase of approximately 25% over its present volume.

Of the eleven Class I forwarders [2] which serve Texas, three lack sufficient traffic to make four cars daily and another is barely able to meet this minimum requirement. In recent years, two forwarders have gone bankrupt attempting to operate to Texas. Similarly, of the seventeen Class I forwarders serving California, three do not have sufficient tonnage to meet the minimum requirement of ten cars weekly.

In addition to the necessity to establish a sufficient number of stations in the west to avoid long, time consuming off-line truck hauls, it is equally necessary that a forwarder maintain a sufficient number of stations in the east to avoid delay in getting freight into a consolidated carload and moving enroute to its ultimate destination. In other words, the forwarder which must truck freight from Pittsburgh to Chicago before it can load it into a car cannot offer as fast a service as the forwarder who is in a position to consolidate carloads of freight at Pittsburgh.

(9) Including both Class I and Class II forwarders, forty-eight freight forwarders are presently authorized to perform westbound service from and to the states covered by the application and twenty-nine freight forwarders are authorized to perform eastbound service from and to such states.

(10) By far the greater portion of the traffic which Lifschultz will be able to obtain for movement in its proposed new service will be diverted from existing freight forwarders.

(11) In many instances existing forwarders serving this territory lack sufficient tonnage to provide a service which meets even the minimum requirements. In some cases even the larger forwarders are barely able to maintain an

---

[2] Forwarders having a gross revenue of $100,000 per year or more.

adequate service, particularly to and from smaller communities. Loss of traffic to Lifschultz seriously threatens to impair or curtail these forwarders' services.

The Issues

The issues before the Interstate Commerce Commission and before the District Court were:

(1) Whether there was substantial evidence to support the Interstate Commerce Commission's conclusions that the proposed freight forwarder service would be consistent with the public interest and the National Transportation Policy;

(2) Whether the ultimate conclusion of the Interstate Commerce Commission was sufficiently supported by basic findings of fact; and

(3) Whether Section 410(d) of the Interstate Commerce Act excuses an applicant for a freight forwarder permit from the burden of sustaining the several elements of proof affirmatively imposed by Section 410(c) of that Act.

Conclusions of the Interstate Commerce Commission

With one or two important exceptions, hereinafter noted, the conclusions of fact which were reached by the Interstate Commerce Commission are substantially correct. In and of themselves these findings of fact are relatively innocuous. The outstandingly significant defect in the Commission's decision lies in the facts which it did not find and in the arbitrary and capricious manner in which it weighed and evaluated the evidence.

The Commission found that to and from the States of Minnesota, Texas and California applicant's proposed services are desired and would be used by certain shippers. This finding undoubtedly is correct as far as it goes. The

Commission did not attempt to find the *extent* to which these shippers would utilize applicant's service.

The Commission found that Lifschultz has been in operation since 1899, has numerous experienced employees and has operated at a profit. This finding is undoubtedly correct.

When the Commission's report is stripped of all non-essential verbiage, these are the only two essential, affirmative findings contained therein in support of the Commission's order.

The Interstate Commerce Act affirmatively imposes a duty upon the Commission to find that certain conditions have been met before it authorizes the issuance of a freight forwarder permit. These requirements are set forth in Section 410(c) of the Act. They are (1) that an applicant must be ready, able and willing properly to perform the service proposed and (2) that the proposed service is or will be consistent with the public interest and the National Transportation Policy.

The Commission is required affirmatively to find that these conditions have been met and the burden of proving that these conditions have been met rests with the applicant who seeks a permit.[3]

The standard of consistency with public interest and the National Transportation Policy has clearly defined meaning, not only by the specific provisions of the statute but by past decisions of the courts and the Commission. In *New York Central Securities Corporation* v. *U. S.*, 287 U. S. 12, 23, the Supreme Court held that:

> "The public interest is served by economy and efficiency in operation. . . ."

---

[3] *Carloader Corporation, Freight Forwarder Application,* 260 ICC 401; *Bernstein Service Freight Forwarder Application,* 260 ICC 498; *Clipper Carloading Corporation,* 260 ICC 818, 830.

"It is a mistaken assumption that this (the criterion of 'public interest') is a mere general reference to public welfare without any standard to guide determinations. The purpose of the Act, the requirements it imposes and the context of the provisions in question show the contrary. Going forward from a policy mainly directed to the prevention of abuses, particularly those arising from excessive or discriminatory rates, Transportation Act 1920, was designed better to insure adequacy in transportation service. * * * The provisions now before us were among the additions made by Transportation Act 1920 and the term 'public interest' thus used is not a concept without ascertainable criteria, but has direct relation to adequacy of transportation service, to its essential conditions of economy and efficiency, and to appropriate provision and best use of transportation facilities * * * ."

Likewise in *Worm Extension-Ainsworth and Johnstown, Nebraska,* 32 MCC 641-644, the Interstate Commerce Commission held:

"The term 'consistent with the public interest' means not against or contradictory to the public interest, and it must be considered in connection with the national transportation policy of Congress, which places emphasis upon the maintenance of safe, adequate, economical and efficient service, sound economic conditions in transportation, and the preservation of a national transportation system adequate to meet the needs of commerce."

"The prime element in determining the public interest is the maintenace of adequate transportation facilities for handling general traffic. It may be that some individual shipper may find it more convenient or more economical to have a contract carrier handle for him a particular kind of traffic. This, however, does not constitute a conclusive test. If taking that traffic from the established transportation agencies may so reduce their earnings that they will be unable to maintain

adequate and efficient common carrier service for the
public including that individual, then it is not in the
public interest.''

But we need not rely upon these decisions which represent judicial and administrative interpretation of the language of the statute. The statute itself is explicit. The
National Transportation Policy commands the Interstate
Commerce Commission to so administer the Act as to recognize and preserve the inherent advantages of each mode
of transportation; to promote safe, adequate, economical
and efficient service and foster sound economic conditions
in transportation and among the several carriers. Not only
does Section 410(c) specifically require the Commission
to find that a proposed forwarder service will be consistent
with the above named standards, but the National Transportation Policy itself concludes by providing that ''all of
the provisions of this Act shall be administered and enforced with a view to carrying out the above declaration of
policy.''

Ultimately, therefore, the plain meaning of the statute
is that before it may authorize the issuance of a freight
forwarder permit, the Commission must find as a fact that
the service proposed will be conducive to the maintenance
of adequate, economical and efficient forwarder service.

The findings of the Commission that Lifschultz is an experienced and successful operator and that a few shippers
would use its proposed service to some unspecified extent
do not meet this test.

Certain evidence of record which the Commission did not
even mention in its report, and which it apparently disregarded, shows that operating conditions in the West are
substantially different than in the East where Lifschultz
now operates. This evidence shows that the distances between cities are much greater in the West than in the East;

that population density is less and that traffic is dispersed over wider geographical areas. It also shows that the railroad rate structure is basically different in the West than in the East requiring a substantially larger volume of tonnage to permit efficient and successful freight forwarding operations. The mere facts that Lifschultz has operated successfully in the East, and that a few shippers may use its service (although their testimony did not indicate that they had any substantial amount of tonnage to offer) do not show that Lifschultz will be able to overcome these operating difficulties in the West and provide an adequate, efficient and economical service.

The record shows that many freight forwarders now serving the States of Texas and California are unable to obtain a sufficient volume of business to overcome these difficulties and operate efficiently and economically. The record shows that within recent years two freight forwarders have gone bankrupt attempting to serve the State of Texas.

Lifschultz offered no testimony addressed to this problem and the record is completely devoid of evidence as to where Lifschultz will operate, how it will operate or what volume of tonnage it may reasonably expect to handle.

Under Parts I, II, or III the Commission unquestionably would deny an application for a permit or a certificate which was so deficient with respect to these essential considerations. Yet, under Part IV the Commission has concluded that it was the policy of Congress that freight forwarder permits should be issued freely. The Commission has given effect to this concept of liberality by failing to require of this applicant the essential elements of proof which would normally be required and which, we submit, are required under Section 410(c). This failure on the part of the Commission to require substantial evidence in support of the application has a two-fold effect. Not only does it excuse the applicant from proving that its proposed service will be adequate, economical, and efficient in conformity with the National Transportation Policy but it precludes the protestants from effectively proving the contrary.

Having been confronted with no specific proposal these appellants (protestants before the Commission) were unable to prove specifically wherein they or the public would be injured if the proposed service were instituted. The evidence offered by these protestants showed that a forwarder who lacked sufficient tonnage to consolidate cars at numerous stations throughout the East and to ship those cars to numerous stations throughout the West would necessarily have to resort to long, off-line truck hauls to and from its consolidation and distribution stations, which would result in a slower and less efficient service than the public normally expects and receives from freight forwarders. The evidence showed that from and to many smaller communities existing forwarders have difficulty maintaining direct car service because the tonnage available for movement to and from such communities is relatively small. Thus the loss of even a few thousand pounds would seriously threaten to impair this service by making it impossible for existing forwarders to accumulate and ship carload consignments of freight as frequently as they do at present. The evidence showed that even between the larger cities many smaller forwarders are barely able to attract sufficient tonnage to maintain an acceptable standard of service. The loss of even a small amount of tonnage would impair these forwarders' service by making it impossible for them to accumulate and ship consolidated carload consignments with the necessary frequency. When it is borne in mind that speed in transit is the primary economic utility of the freight forwarder, it will be seen that any forwarder service which does not offer the public at least the normally accepted time in transit, or which by diverting freight from other forwarders brings about a reduction in the frequency of their service, is not consistent with the public interest and the National Transportation Policy. The Commission conceded this to be true but held that protestants had not sufficiently proven that the proposed new service would have this effect. Thus, by this process of administrative reasoning, protestants were indeed cast upon the horns of dilemma. Pursuant to a policy of liberality, the applicant was not required to prove where or how it would operate. Pursuant to the same policy of liberality, protestants were told in effect that they must prove specifically where and how that operation would adversely affect the public. Thus, an operation which may well be intrinsically inefficient or uneconomical, and which seriously threatens to impair existing forwarder service to the public has been approved, although the record contains not one scintilla of evidence tending to show that these undesirable consequences will not result, and contains substantial evidence that such consequences are likely and probable.

To illustrate further, had this applicant testified that it would serve Austin, Texas by stopping off cars destined to San Antonio, it could have been shown in rebuttal that its service to San Antonio would thereby be delayed for one day. Had this applicant testified that it proposed to serve San Angelo, Texas by joint loading with another forwarder to Dallas, it could have been shown that its service to San Angelo would be at least two or three days slower than the prevailing standards of forwarder service. Had this applicant testified that it would obtain sufficient tonnage to serve Odessa or Abilene or Lubbock or Beaumont or Tyler, Texas it could have been shown that such tonnage would come from existing forwarders and would impair the quality of their service to those points.

Primarily, the Commission should have denied the application because it was unsupported by any evidence tending to show that the proposed service would be adequate, efficient or economical. In the alternative, since it accepted such vague and generalized evidence in support of the application, the Commission should have accorded equal weight to the necessarily general testimony which was offered in rebuttal. Unless the Commission is required to adopt one of these alternatives the standards imposed by Section 410(c) will be completely vitiated. If an applicant for permit is not to be required to tell what it proposes to do and how it proposes to do it, and if at the same time, evidence tending to show that the proposed service would be inconsistent with the public interest and the National Transportation Policy is required to be detailed and specific, then freight forwarder permits will issue as a matter of course to every applicant for they will be required to make no proof and the parties adversely affected will have no effective means of resisting the application.

The liberal policy which the Commission has adopted must of necessity stem from Section 410(d) of the Act. The provisions of Section 410(c) are substantially the same as the corresponding provisions which appear in Parts II and III. The only difference which appears in Part IV, and therefore the only basis for adopting a different interpretation of Part IV, is Section 410(d). This section provides that no application for a permit shall be denied solely because the service proposed will be competitive with the services of existing forwarders.

When the Freight Forwarder Act was passed, Rep. Wolverton discussed this provision at some length on the floor of the House. From this provision of the Act, and from the legislative history embodied in Rep. Wolverton's remarks, the Commission has drawn the inference that Congress intended freight forwarder permits to be issued liberally. While it undoubtedly is true that to the extent that Section 410(d) modifies Section 410(c), greater liberality was intended than under other parts of the Act which do not contain such a limitation, the Commission has carried this policy of liberality far beyond the reasonable requirements of Section 410(d). When the Freight Forwarder Act was under consideration in the Congress, the version originally passed by the Senate would have imposed the test of public convenience and necessity as a prerequisite to the issuance of a certificate. The House version imposed the more liberal requirement of proof of consistency with the public interest and the national transportation policy, and added Section 410(d), further limiting the grounds upon which an application might be denied. Therefore, when the bill was reported upon the floor of the House, Rep. Wolverton undertook to explain *"the reasons which impelled your Committee to recommend the differences that appear"* (87 Daily Congressional Record 8426, October 23, 1941). In other words, all that Rep. Wolverton undertook to do was to explain why the language which appears in Sections 410(c) and 410(d) was adopted rather than the more rigorous requirements which had appeared in the Senate bill.

Rep. Wolverton had introduced and undertaken to obtain consideration of an even more liberal measure, H.R. 5179, 77th Congress, 1st Session. Rep. Wolverton's bill contained, in Section 407(d) thereof, the language which appears in Section 410(d) but did not include the important word, "solely." When the bill was referred to the House Committee on Interstate and Foreign Commerce *the Committee as a whole agreed to the limitation only after it had inserted the word "solely."* It was in this form that the bill finally passed. Bill H.R. 5179 represented the views of Rep. Wolverton, but the Congress as a whole adopted something entirely different. This shows conclusively that on this point the views of the Congress as a whole were not as liberal as those of Rep. Wolverton. In giving his explanation to the Congress in remarks on the floor, Rep.

Wolverton pointedly omitted using the word "solely," but the Committee Report gives the word prominence (H. Rep. 1172, 77th Cong., 1st Session). Yet the Commission apparently has adopted the view that Rep. Wolverton's remarks proceed from Sections 410(c) and 410(d) as a starting point and indicate that an even more liberal interpretation of the Act is required than is self-evident from the language of the statute. This construction ignores the fact that the Committee had already considered this point and that the language enacted represented the collective views of the Committee and the Congress as to the standards to be applied.

Therefore, wholly apart from the facts of the case which admittedly are complicated and technical in that they deal with the mechanics of freight forwarder operation, the Commission's basic error is one of law. Primarily, the Commission has concluded that freight forwarder permits should be issued freely. To that end it has so relaxed the standards of proof required of an applicant and has imposed such a strict requirement of proof upon those who oppose the granting of an application as to preclude any realistic weighing and evaluation of the merits of the parties' contentions and to make meaningless the procedures of hearing and argument. If an application may be granted without substantial evidence *with respect to the basic issues involved,* and if those who oppose the application can hope to prevail only by rebutting specifically, proposals which are inherently vague and unspecific, then the process of a hearing before the Commission becomes a mere futility.

Findings and Conclusions of the Three-Judge Court

Following argument on the merits and the filing of briefs, the U. S. District Court for the Northern District of Illinois, Eastern Division, issued a decree on April 27,

1949 denying the relief requested by appellants (plaintiffs below) and dismissing the suit. The court's decree was supported by Findings of Fact and Conclusions of Law. The court's Findings of Fact, Conclusions of Law and Decree are attached hereto and made a part hereof.

The court did not discuss and apparently did not consider the basic error of law set forth above. Instead, it held briefly that the Commission's order was supported by substantial evidence, that it was supported by the necessary essential findings of fact, and that it was not arbitrary or unreasonable. We respectfully submit that these conclusions of the court are erroneous both in fact and in law.

The Question Presented Is Substantial

There is here presented for the first time the question of construction and interpretation of Sections 310(c) and 410(d) of Part IV of the Interstate Commerce Act. These sections combined form one of the most essential provisions of Part IV for they deal with the subject of enfranchisement. The whole subject matter of Part IV is the regulation of freight forwarders and these two sections vest the Interstate Commerce Commission with power to determine who shall be regulated and who may engage in business as a freight forwarder. Thus, these sections, in a sense, control the creation of the subject matter to which the remainder of Part IV applies.

The construction of these two sections is of vital importance for another reason. The most essential economic characteristic of freight forwarding is the concentration and channelization of traffic. The reason that freight forwarder service is superior to railroad less than carload service and the reason that it is patronized so extensively by the shipping public is that through the channelization of traffic movements into relatively few routes, far greater speed and efficiency is achieved than can be achieved when traffic is thinly dispersed over hundreds of different routes, no one of which enjoys a sufficient volume to permit the use of through cars and the other efficiencies which are inherent in large scale operations. This is an inherent advantage of freight forwarding and one which the National Transportation Policy commands the Commission to recognize and preserve. Yet, through its liberal policy of issuing freight forwarder permits, pursuant to its erroneous construction of the statute, the Commission has destroyed this inherent advantage. By creating an infinite number of forwarder routes the Commission is encouraging the dispersion and diffusion of fordwarder traffic which is the very antithesis of the concentration and channelization which is essential to efficient and economical freight forwarding operations. For example, in 1938 the Commission found that there were some twenty freight forwarders in existence.[4] At the present time the Commission has issued well over 100 freight forwarder permits and the record in this proceeding shows that within the territory covered by this application 48 freight forwarders are now authorized to operate west bound and 29 east bound.

The number of freight forwarder permits which have been granted is more than sufficient to assure the public of an abundance of forwarder service and to meet any reasonable requirement of effective competition within the industry. Hereafter, the only effect which the authorization of new forwarder service can have will be to reduce the speed and frequency of existing service through diffusion of the total available quantity of traffic among more freight forwarders than are economically justified.

We respectfully submit that the construction which the Interstate Commerce Commission has placed upon these provisions of the statute amounts in effect to denial of the

---

[4] *Freight Forwarding Investigation,* 229 ICC 201, 203.

safeguards which the Congress undertook to impose in Section 410(c). These safeguards are for the benefit of the public as well as for the benefit of the regulated freight forwarders. Such safeguards are an inherent characteristic of public utility regulation. Customarily, wherever a utility is deprived of the right to conduct its business freely and in accordance with the dictates of its own judgment, including the right to engage in competitive warfare, and is subjected to regulation, it is accorded protection against destructive competition against which it has been rendered powerless adequately to protect itself. Such was the purpose of Section 410(c). Similar provisions in Parts I, II, and III of the Act have been thus construed and enforced. Yet here the Commission has construed the provisions of Section 410(c) almost as if they did not exist and the mere filing of an application would appear to constitute sufficient grounds in the judgment of the Commission to authorize the issuance of a permit. If the public and the regulated freight forwarding industry are to be accorded the protection which they require, to which they are entitled, and which the Congress intended to confer, Section 410(c) must be given a more realistic construction and must be more realistically applied and enforced than the construction and application manifested by the Commission's report and order in this proceeding. We respectfully submit, therefore, that a substantial and vital question is presented by this appeal which calls for the appropriate exercise of appellate jurisdiction.

Respectfully submitted,

DAVID AXELROD,
JAMES L. GIVAN,
Attorneys for Plaintiffs.

Dated June 24, 1949.

APPENDIX A

IN THE DISTRICT COURT OF THE UNITED STATES
FOR THE NORTHERN DISTRICT OF ILLINOIS
EASTERN DIVISION

Civil Action No. 49C 409

ACME FAST FREIGHT, INC. ET AL., *Plaintiffs,*

v.

UNITED STATES OF AMERICA AND INTERSTATE COMMERCE
COMMISSION, *Defendants*

FINDINGS OF FACT

The Court makes the following findings of fact:

1. The Interstate Commerce Commission, on September 16, 1948, filed its report and order in Docket No. FF-95, FF-95 (Sub-No. 1), and FF-95 (Sub-No. 2), in which it granted to Lifschultz Fast Freight, a partnership having its principal place of business in Chicago, Illinois, a permit authorizing extension of operations as a freight forwarder of commodities generally, except when imported or consigned for export, in interstate commerce, between points in Milwaukee, Waukesha, Jefferson, Dane, Iowa, Grant, Lafayette, Green, Rock, Walworth, Racine, and Kenosha Counties, Wisconsin; Lake County, Indiana, and in Illinois in and north of the counties of Adams, Brown, Cass, Menard, Logan, DeWitt, Piatt, Champaign, and Vermillion; and in Iowa along the west bank of the Mississippi River from Dubuque to Keokuk, inclusive, on the one hand, and those in Minnesota, Texas, and California, on the other hand.

2. The application of Lifschultz Fast Freight, seeking extension of authority to operate between points in, and north and east of, Maryland, Pennsylvania, Ohio, Indiana, Illinois, and Wisconsin, on the one hand, and those in Minnesota, North Dakota, Texas, New Mexico, Arizona,

Nevada and California, on the other hand, had been assigned for hearings before two Commission examiners who made detailed findings of fact and recommended that authority be granted applicant to operate between the Illinois, Iowa, Indiana and Wisconsin Territory described in paragraph 1 above, on the one hand, and points in Minnesota, Texas and California, on the other hand. A division of the Commission considered the recommended report and made one of its own, containing findings of fact and numerous subsidiary findings in support of its order granting applicant a permit as recommended in the examiner's report, except for the limitation imposed in respect of domestic traffic. Petitions for reconsideration were denied, and the final order of the Commission was entered, superseding and cancelling the prior orders authorizing applicant's present operations, and incorporated that authority in the final order designated "Third Amended Permit and Order," which granted the expanded authority as prayed to the extent heretofore described.

3. The Commission has found that service by applicant as a freight forwarder of commodities generally (except when imported or consigned for export) in interstate commerce, between the points noted above, will be consistent with the public interest and the national transportation policy, and that applicant is ready, able and willing to perform such service, and has supported this ultimate finding of fact by findings of evidentiary facts which support the ultimate finding.

4. That the findings of the Commission are supported by substantial evidence and are not arbitrary, or unreasonable.

CONCLUSIONS OF LAW

And the Court sets forth the following as its conclusions of law:

1. The Commission was acting within the proper limits of its discretion in holding that the grant of a permit to applicant in extension of its freight forwarder service will be consistent with the public interest and the national

transportation policy and that applicant is ready, able and willing to perform such service.

2. The order of the Commission granting the permit to applicant is a legal and valid order.

3. Injunction should be denied and the suit should be dismissed.

(S.) J. EARL MAJOR,
Chief Judge,
Circuit Court of Appeals,
(S.) JOHN P. BARNES,
United States District Judge,
(S.) PHILIP L. SULLIVAN,
United States District Judge.

APPENDIX B

IN THE DISTRICT COURT OF THE UNITED STATES FOR THE NORTHERN DISTRICT OF ILLINOIS EASTERN DIVISION

Civil Action No. 49C 409

ACME FAST FREIGHT, INC. ET AL., *Plaintiffs,*

v.

UNITED STATES OF AMERICA AND INTERSTATE COMMERCE COMMISSION, *Defendants*

DECREE

This cause coming on to be heard before the undersigned, constituting a special District Court of three judges convened pursuant to 28 U.S.C.A. 2484(1), and 2325, upon an application for an interlocutory injunction; and being heard upon the evidence taken before the Interstate Commerce Commission and the Report of the Commission, as well as upon the arguments and briefs of counsel; and the cause, by consent of the parties, having been submitted for final decree; and the Court having made its findings of fact and conclusions of law which are filed herewith:

Now, therefore, upon the basis of such findings of fact and conclusions of law, it is ordered, adjudged and decreed that the injunction and other relief prayed for in the complaint be denied and that the suit be dismissed.

This 27th day of April, 1949.

(S.) J. EARL MAJOR,
Chief Judge,
Circuit Court of Appeals,
(S.) JOHN P. BARNES,
United States District Judge,
(S.) PHILIP L. SULLIVAN,
United States District Judge.

(4310)

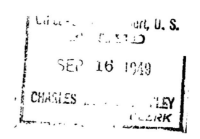

No. 338

In the Supreme Court of the United States

OCTOBER TERM, 1949

ACME FAST FREIGHT, INC., ET AL., APPELLANTS

vs.

THE UNITED STATES OF AMERICA, INTERSTATE COM-
MERCE COMMISSION, ET AL.

---

*APPEAL FROM THE UNITED STATES DISTRICT COURT
FOR THE NORTHERN DISTRICT OF ILLINOIS*

MOTION TO AFFIRM

IN THE UNITED STATES DISTRICT COURT FOR THE NORTHERN DISTRICT OF ILLINOIS

CIVIL No. 49 C 409

ACME FAST FREIGHT, INC., ET AL., PLAINTIFFS-APPEL-
LANTS

v.

UNITED STATES OF AMERICA, AND INTERSTATE COM-
MERCE COMMISSION, DEFENDANTS-APPELLEES

MOTION TO AFFIRM

Appellees, pursuant to Rule 12, paragraph 3, of the Revised Rules of the Supreme Court of the United States, move that the judgment and decree of the District Court be affirmed.

This is a direct appeal from the final judgment and decree, entered on April 27, 1949 [1] by a specially constituted district court of three judges established pursuant to Sections 2284 and 2325, Title 28 of the United States Code, dismissing appellants' complaint seeking to set aside an order of the Interstate Commerce Commission. Appeal was allowed on June 24, 1949, and appeal papers were served on June 29, 1949.

---

[1] The court entered no opinion, but made and entered findings of fact and conclusions of law on April 27, 1949. On May 23, 1949 the District Court, after hearing argument, denied appellant's application for stay pending appeal. The Commission's order became effective May 31, 1949.

The Commission's order,[2] dated September 16, 1948, granted Lifschultz Fast Freight (hereinafter sometimes referred to as Lifschultz or the applicant) authority to extend its operations as a freight forwarder[3] in interstate commerce between specified areas in the United States as more fully described in said report and order. In an earlier proceeding and by a permit issued in 1945, Lifschultz had been authorized to operate between

---

[2] The order in terms authorized Lifschultz Fast Freight "to operate, in interstate commerce, as a freight forwarder (1) of commodities generally, between points in Maryland and Pennsylvania and points in the United States north and east thereof, on the one hand, and on the other, points in Milwaukee, Waukesha, Jefferson, Dane, Iowa, Grant, Lafayette, Greene, Rock, Walworth, Racine, and Kenosha Counties, Wis., Lake County, Ind., and in Illinois in and north of the Counties of Adams, Brown, Cass, Menard, Logan, DeWitt, Piatt, Champaign, and Vermilion, and in Iowa along the west bank of the Mississippi River from Dubuque to Keokuk, inclusive, and (2) of commodities generally (except when imported or consigned for export) between the points in Illinois, Indiana, Iowa and Wisconsin, described in (1) above, on the one hand, those in Minnesota, Texas and California, on the other . . ."

[3] As defined in Section 402 of the Interstate Commerce Act (49 U. S. C. 1002):

The term "freight forwarder" means any person which (otherwise than as a carrier subject to Part I, II, or III of this Act) holds itself out to the general public to transport or provide transportation of property, or any class or classes of property, for compensation, in interstate commerce, and which in the ordinary and usual course of its undertaking, (A) assembles and consolidates or provides for assembling and consolidating, shipments, and (B) assumes responsibility for the transportation of such property from point of receipt to point of destination and (C) utilizes for the whole or any part of the transportation of such shipments, the services of a carrier or carriers subject to Part I, II, or III of this Act.

For a full description of freight forwarder practices, see *United States* v. *Chicago Heights Trucking Co.,* 310 U. S. 344; *Chicago, M., St. Paul and Pac. R. Co. et al.,* v. *Acme Fast Freight, Inc.,* 336 U. S. 465; *Freight Forwarding Investigation,* 229 I. C. C. 201; *Bills of Lading of Freight Forwarders,* 259 I. C. C. 277.

points in, and north and east of, Maryland and Pennsylvania, on the one hand, and those in portions of Wisconsin, Indiana, Illinois, and Iowa, on the other.

Appellants, who are freight forwarders (some having nation-wide operating authority), generally in competition with Lifschultz, appeared as protestants before the Commission and opposed the granting of the authority sought by the applicant. Appellants contended there as they contended in the District Court, and as they now contend here, that the order of the Commission is unlawful and void because contrary to the statutory standards for freight forwarder operations as set out in sections 410 (c) and 410 (d) of the Interstate Commerce Act (49 U. S. C. 1010 (c) and 1010 (d)),[4] and that the order is unsupported by substantial evidence and lacking in essential findings.

Appellees submit that this appeal involves no substantial questions. Appellants' arguments as revealed by their Jurisdictional Statement are

---

[4] The provisions of said sections are as follows:

Section 410 (c), (49 U. S. C. 1010 (c)):

The Commission shall issue a permit to any qualified applicant therefor, authorizing the whole or any part of the service covered by the application if the Commission finds that the applicant is ready, able, and willing properly to perform the service proposed, and that the proposed service to the extent authorized by the permit, is or will be consistent with the public interest and the national transportation policy declared in this Act; otherwise such application shall be denied.

Section 410 (d), (49 U. S. C. 1010 (d)):

The Commission shall not deny authority to engage in the whole or any part of the proposed service covered by any application made under this section solely on the ground that such service will be in competition with the service subject to this part performed by any other freight forwarder or freight forwarders.

simply reiterations of arguments previously re-
jected by the Commission and the District Court,
addressed mainly to matters lying within the discretion of the Commission. Appellants admit [5]
that the conclusions reached by the Commission
are substantially correct, with one or two alleged
important exceptions. They explain that the significant defect in the Commission's decision is its
failure to find additional facts, and the arbitrary
and capricious manner in which it weighed and
evaluated the evidence.

Pursuant to section 410 (c), the Commission is
authorized to grant permits of the type involved in
this proceeding if it "finds that the applicant is
ready, able, and willing properly to perform the
service proposed." As to this requirement the Commission found that:

> Applicant's readiness and ability to perform
> the service is not questioned. The long experi-
> ence of applicant and its predecessors, and its
> financial condition, together with other evi-
> dence of record, establish that it is ready and
> able to perform the service for which au-
> thority is granted. (265 I. C. C. 431, 445)

As revealed by their Jurisdictional Statement, appellants admit that there is evidence in the record
to support these findings by the Commission.[6] It
must be concluded that any attack upon the Commission's findings with respect the question of
readiness, ability, and willingness to perform the
service proposed runs squarely against repeated

---

[5] Page 6, Jurisdictional Statement (references are to mimeographed copy; "Conclusions of the Interstate Commerce Commission").

[6] Page 3, Jurisdictional Statement ("The Facts of the
Case").

enunciation by this Court that once it is established that the findings of the Commission have substantial support in the evidence and provide a rational basis for the conclusion reached, they are unassailable in a proceeding of this type. *Interstate Commerce Commission* v. *Union Pacific Railroad Co.,* 222 U. S. 541, 547; *Virginian R. Co.* v. *United States,* 272 U. S. 658, 665; *Mississippi Valley Barge Line* v. *United States,* 292 U. S. 282, 286, 287.; *Rochester Telephone Corp.* v. *United States,* 207 U. S. 125, 146; *United States* v. *Carolina Freight Carriers Corp.,* 315 U. S. 475, 482, 490.

The second and only remaining finding necessary to support the Commission's order is "that the proposed service to the extent authorized by the permit, is or will be consistent with the public interest and the national transportation policy" declared in the Act.

The phrase "consistent with the public interest and the national transportation policy" has been used in several sections of the Act as a standard to guide the discretion imposed in the Commission when it acts upon applications for various types of authority. Admittedly [7] a more liberal standard than that of public convenience and necessity required in the case of many other types of operating authority, it is nevertheless a standard which requires the Commission to give consideration to the transportation needs of the public, the necessity of enlarging transportation facilities, and measures which would best promote the service in the interest of the public and the commerce of the people. *New York Central Securities Corp.* v. *United*

---

[7] This is also the view of appellants, page 11, Jurisdictional Statement) ("Conclusions of the Interstate Commerce Commission").

States, 287 U. S. 12, 23-25. *McLean Trucking Co.*
v. *United States,* 321 U. S. 67, 81-82.

In support of its determination that the authority
granted "will be consistent with the public interest
and the national transportation policy . . ." (265
I. C. C. 431, 445), the Commission specifically
found that:

> The shippers supporting the application use
> applicant's service between Chicago and points
> in trunk-line and New England territories.
> They have received more prompt pick-up serv-
> ice and earlier delivery from applicant than
> from other forwarders. In addition, its efficient
> trading and claim-adjustment services have
> contributed to their preference for applicant.
> They anticipate similar advantage through use
> of the extended service here proposed, and
> their support is prompted by this considera-
> tion. (265 I. C. C. 431, 433-434).
>
> Witnesses supporting the application are
> shipping between the points here involved by
> rail, truck, express, and air, as well as by
> freight forwarders. Their desire for appli-
> cant's proposed service warrants the infer-
> ences that they would ship some part of their
> traffic in that service. Upon cross-examina-
> tion, however, they state that the services of
> existing forwarders have been generally satis-
> factory. (265 I. C. C. 431, 434).

Again we note that appellants agree (page 3,
Jurisdictional Statement) that there is evidence
in the record to support these findings. It should
therefore be concluded that the Commission has
complied with the provisions of the Act and made
the basic findings necessary to support its action,
and that the record furnishes substantial evidence
in support of such findings. It is pertinent to note
in this respect that "The judicial function is ex-

hausted when there is found to be a rational basis
for the conclusions approved by the administrative
body." *Rochester Tel. Corp.* v. *United States,* 307
U. S. 125, 146; *Mississippi Valley Barge Line* v.
United States, 292 U. S. 282, 286-287.

Appellants' remaining argument in support of
its contention that the applicant failed to prove
that its new operation is or will be consistent with
the public interest and the national transportation
policy, directs attention to the alleged significant
omission by the applicant of a detailed description
of its proposed plan of operations including the
location of terminal (assembling and distributing)
points, and prophecies as to anticipated tonnage
to specific destinations. It is apparent that by
such an argument appellants seek to twist this proceeding into one analogous to one for a certificate
of public convenience and necessity. Such an
argument also completely ignores the unique nature of freight forwarder operations. The routes
that the traffic will follow are, of course, the routes
established by the carriers whose services the applicant will use. The volume of tonnage moved
over a particular route by Lifschultz will, of course,
depend in part on the individual enterprise and
ability of Lifschultz in continuing to retain and
add to the number of persons using its services.
The tonnage also will be variable in consideration
of the sales of such users. It is true that when
the Commission is passing on applications for certificates of public convenience and necessity in the
motor or water carrier fields, it is important that
it obtain specific information as to the requirements of the public for the additional service, together with specific information as to the routes or
territories sought to be served by the carrier. It is

clear, however, that these requirements are not applicable to freight forwarders, whose operations do not require investments in terminal stations, rolling stock or other equipment. It was for these reasons that the requirement that freight forwarder obtain certificates of public convenience and necessity incorporated by the United States Senate in its draft of the bill which was to become the Freight Forwarder Act was stricken from the bill when it was enacted into law.[8]

Appellants' final argument is a restatement of their contention before the Commission and the District Court, to the effect that the operations of the applicant in the territory granted would create a diffusion of traffic between forwarders with a resulting lack of speed and efficiency on the part of all forwarders. Such an argument is, of course, one addressed solely to the matter of competition. It is clear that such argument runs squarely into the specific limitation imposed on the Commission by Section 410 (d) of the Act which provides in substance that:

> The Commission shall not deny authority to engage in the whole or any part of the proposed service covered by any application made under this section solely on the ground that such service will be in competition with the

---

[8] The matter of the scope of authority to be given the Commission, and the standards furnished to guide its determinations, received detailed consideration by Congress at the time of passage of the Freight Forwarder Act. For the convenience of the Court pertinent excerpts from the legislative history of the Act have been set out in Appendix I, included herewith.

service subject to this part performed by any other freight forwarder or freight forwarders.[9]

The Commission gave specific consideration to this argument of appellants, and while finding it was not relevant, being thus addressed to the matter of competition, it found also that appellants had failed to prove their contentions. In this regard, it noted:

> While protestants' witnesses are of the view that service by applicant would divert traffic from forwarders at present serving these territories, they do not undertake to estimate the amount of diversion. In any event, such estimates would of necessity have been highly speculative. On this record, the most we can say is that there would be some diversion of traffic, but it is impossible to form any reliable estimate as to the probable extent thereof. This conclusion was reached also in the proposed report.[10] (265 I. C. C. 431, 442)

---

[9] Descriptive of the legislative intent in enacting the specific provisions of Section 410 (d) are the remarks of Representative Wolverton that:

> The provision in paragraph (d) of section 410, to the effect that no application for a permit shall be denied because of the existence of other forwarder service which would be competitive, is predicated upon the essential nature of forwarder service, so far as the actual carriers are concerned. *Without such a provision, there might be a tendency to deny legitimate operations on the ground that the existing forwarder service was adequate.* The Committee was of the opinion that if the advantages of freight forwarder service are as great as are claimed for it, then the greatest opportunity should be given to persons to go into the business and to make it available to the public to the greatest extent possible. (Italics furnished) (87 Cong. Rec. 8220).

[10] At this point the Commission referred to an earlier proceeding wherein one of the present protestants made a similar allegation. Noting that there the allegation failed of proof even though the record disclosed that service had been actually

From the evidence submitted by applicant, it appears that, to the extent indicated above, applicant's proposed services are desired and would be used by certain shippers. It is not incumbent upon applicant to show that its proposed operation would not impair existing service. Applicant is in no position to make such showing. Although the extension of applicant's service probably would result in some further diffusion of the existing volume of traffic, it cannot be said that this would of necessity result in reduced frequency of service. The practice has long obtained of two or more freight forwarders loading their shipments together, in the same car, in order thereby to have sufficient tonnage to make up a carload. See for example *Kelly Freight Forwarder Application,* 260 I. C. C. 315. By participating in such coloading of traffic the individual forwarder is relieved of the necessity of holding its shipments for accumulation of a minimum carload of its own, and it is thereby enabled to dispatch shipments more frequently than otherwise would be feasible. This practice is so general that it was accorded specific recognition and sanction in part IV of the Act, and regulations have been promulgated by this Commission concerning the making and filing of joint-loading contracts. (265 I. C. C. 442-443)

---

instituted by the applicant prior to the Commission proceeding, it said:

If in *International Forwarding Co. F. F. Application, supra,* [260 I. C. C. 249, 253], Acme was unable to show, after International's service to Texas had been instituted and had been conducted over a period of time, that it had been adversely affected thereby, we cannot say that a more explicit description of applicant's proposed plan of operations would any better enable Acme to show the probable effect of the proposed service. (265 I. C. C. 431, 442)

It has thus been shown that the Commission, after carefully considering all the arguments raised by appellants, found that the applicant was ready, able, and willing to perform the service proposed, and that the authority granted is or will be consistent with the public interest and the national transportation policy. Such findings when supported by substantial evidence are unassailable in an action of this nature. As stated in *United States* v. *Pierce Auto Freight Lines, Inc.,* 327 U. S. 515, 535-536, it is not true that the courts must in a litigated case be the arbiters of the paramount public interest. This is rather the business of the Commission, made such by the very terms of the statute. *United States* v. *Detroit & Cleveland Navigation Co.,* 326 U. S. 236, 240-241; *Interstate Commerce Commission* v. *Parker,* 326 U. S. 60, 65; *American Trucking Associations, Inc.* v. *United States,* 326 U. S. 77, 86. The District Court unanimously sustained the findings of the Commission.

For the foregoing reasons, it is evident that this appeal presents no substantial questions. It is therefore respectfully submitted that the decree of the District Court should be affirmed.

PHILIP B. PERLMAN,
Solicitor General.
DANIEL W. KNOWLTON,
Chief Counsel,
Interstate Commerce Commission.
JULY, 1949.

CERTIFICATE OF SERVICE

I certify that a copy of the foregoing motion to affirm was served on counsel for all parties of record by mail this 13th day of July, 1949.

WILLIAM J. HICKEY,
Special Assistant to the Attorney General.

*Pertinent Excerpts from Legislative History of
the Freight Forwarder Act*

(87 Congressional Record 8219)[11]

While the report which accompanies the bill, at
pages 14 and 22, explains the provisions of section
410 concerning permits and the differences between
those provisions and those with respect to certificates of public convenience and necessity as contained in the bill as received from the Senate, the
report gives none of the reasons which impelled
your committee to recommend the differences that
appear. The need for a statement of these reasons
is accentuated by the criticism which certain trucking interests have made of this section.

As received from the Senate the bill contained
provisions for the issuance of certificates of public
convenience and necessity and for special recognition of "grandfather rights" with respect to forwarding operations in existence on July 20, 1937,
the date of the Commission's first decision in the
Acme case (2 M.C.C. 415). Your committee, however, has concluded that the reasons which justify
such provisions in the case of carriers subject to
Part I, II, or III of the Interstate Commerce Act
are not paralleled in the case of forwarders. The
substitute proposed therefor makes provision for
the issuance of permits without reference to any
"grandfather rights."

Some of the differences in the two situations may
be noted. One of the basic reasons for requiring
certificates in the case of carriers which perform a
physical transportation service is predicated upon
the fact that such carriers invest large sums in
plant, facilities, and equipment, and look to the
public to pay rates which shall yield a fair return

---

[11] Remarks by Representative Wolverton, Member of House
Committee on Interstate and Foreign Commerce, who partici-
pated actively in the handling of the bill (see *Chicago, M.
P. & Pac. R. Co.* v. *Acme Fast Freight, Inc.*, 336 U. S. 455).

thereon over and above the costs of operation. It is therefore important that such investments be not made if not needed, and if the result would be to burden the public with unnecessary transportation costs, or by affording an excess of transportation facilities make it unprofitable for existing carriers to operate. Certificates are appropriate in such cases, and their issuance properly restricted to a showing of public convenience and necessity.

The case of the forwarder discloses no comparable situation. He makes no substantial investment in plant, facilities, or equipment, and devotes no material property to the public service. He is primarily a solicitor, consolidator, and shipper of the traffic of others over the transportation lines and facilities of others. The public, therefore, needs no protection against improvident investments by the forwarder in transportation property, facilities, and equipment.

Because forwarders, whether large or small, are essentially shippers in their relation to the carriers whose services they utilize, they properly should acquire no rights by reason of prior operation which would place them in any more favorable a position than any new shipper also desiring to utilize the same carrier services. For this reason your committee has concluded that it would be contrary to sound policy to give special "grandfather" rights to the comparatively few forwarders, to the disadvantage of other shippers seeking to perform similar services.

Some of the truckers have expressed dissatisfaction with the provisions in this section which enable a common carrier under part I, II, or III to own or control a forwarder. They seem to think that a monopoly of forwarding operations would result and that discriminations would be created. Neither of these suppositions is sound. The freedom on the part of anyone to engage in forwarding operations on an equal basis with other forwarders will effectively prevent monopoly, and no discriminations can result under the regulation provided by this bill. It was the absence of such regulation that was responsible for the discriminations found by the Commission in its freight-forwarding investigation (229 I.C.C. 201).

(88 Congressional Record 4067)[12]

One of the most fundamental points of difference between the two bills (original S. 210 and House revised draft) related to the nature of the author-ity which is required to be obtained as a prerequisite to the engaging in forward (sic) operations.

Thus, while sufficient Commission control should be exercised to facilitate appropriate regulation, to provide for registration, and for the filing of rates, keeping of accounts, the making of reports in customary fashion, the House bill contemplated that authority to conduct forwarding operations should be granted by the Commission to all qualified applicants. Under this type of regulation it would not be necessary for an applicant to prove "public convenience and necessity" as required by the Senate bill, but the grant of operating authority would be appropriate without regard to whether the applicant would compete with existing facilities.

Upon careful consideration of the certificate and permit provisions as contained in the Senate and House bills, respectively, the conferees concluded that the House provisions were more appropriate having regard for the peculiar character of forwarding operations. Thus, while certificate provisions are contained in parts I, II, and III of the Interstate Commerce Act, in the case of common carriers by railroad, motor vehicle, and by water, the reasons which were responsible for the certificate provisions as to such carriers do not obtain in the case of freight forwarders. The primary purpose of requiring a certificate as prerequisite to operation is to protect the public from having to

---

[12] Further remarks by Representative Wolverton on the provisions of the bill as reported out of conference, and as enacted into law.

support improvident investments in transportation facilities. Forwarders, however, do not customarily invest any substantial amounts of capital in physical properties or facilities of transportation, but make use of such properties and facilities as may be provided by carriers subject to Part I, II, or III of the Act.

SUPREME COURT OF THE UNITED STATES

OCTOBER TERM, 1949

No. 338

ACME FAST FREIGHT, INC., ET AL.,

Appellants,

vs.

THE UNITED STATES OF AMERICA, INTERSTATE COMMERCE COMMISSION, ET AL.

APPEAL FROM THE UNITED STATES DISTRICT COURT FOR THE NORTHERN DISTRICT OF ILLINOIS

REPLY TO MOTION TO AFFIRM AND SUPPLEMENT THERETO

DAVID AXELROD,
JAMES L. GIVAN,
Counsel for Appellants.

INDEX

Subject Index

Cases Cited

Other Authorities Cited

IN THE DISTRICT COURT OF THE UNITED STATES FOR THE NORTHERN DISTRICT OF ILLINOIS, EASTERN DIVISION

Civil No. 49 C 409

ACME FAST FREIGHT, INC., ET AL.,
Plaintiffs-Appellants,

vs.

UNITED STATES OF AMERICA AND INTERSTATE COMMERCE COMMISSION,
Defendants-Appellees

REPLY TO DEFENDANTS' MOTION TO AFFIRM

Plaintiffs-appellants respectfully submit this, their reply to the motion to affirm filed in the above cause by defendants-appellees on July 13, 1949.

1. This Appeal Presents a Substantial Question

Defendants assert that no substantial question is presented by this appeal since it is addressed primarily to matters within the discretion of the Interstate Commerce Commission and since both the Commission and the District Court already have passed upon the question presented. This contention is without merit. A question is none the less substantial because the administrative agency and the lower court have decided it in the negative. Moreover, neither the Commission nor the court appears to have even considered the basic and fundamental question involved. Certainly it is not within the discretion of the Interstate Commerce Commission to ignore the requirements of the statute and arbitrarily and capriciously act without evidence to support its conclusion, failing to consider substantial evidence which would require a different conclusion to be reached. That is what the Commission has done in this proceeding and the result is not only contrary to the dictates of the statute but is of far-reaching significance to the freight forwarding industry as a whole and to that large segment of the shipping public which depends upon freight forwarder service for the transportation of its goods.

To demonstrate this, it is necessary to consider briefly the economics of freight forwarding.

When a carload lot of freight is tendered to a railroad, that car moves directly from origin to destination without delay at intermediate points along the route. Thus, the large shipper who deals in carload quantities is able to obtain a relatively fast transportation service. For example, a carload shipment moving from New York to Los Angeles or San Francisco, California would arrive on about the eleventh morning following its departure from New York. The smaller shipper who tenders freight to the railroad in less than carload quantities does not receive a comparable service. Less than carload freight is rehandled and transferred from one car to another enroute. As a consequence, a less than carload shipment moving from New York to Los Angeles or San Francisco would take at least twenty days in transit, frequently more. The freight forwarder, by consolidating the less than carload shipments of hundreds of small shippers into carload lots obtains for those small shippers the same expedited service which their larger competitors obtain when they ship in carload quantities. Generally speaking, the freight forwarder does not offer its shippers lower rates than they would have to pay if they shipped in rail less than carload service. The inducement to use forwarder service and the economic value of forwarder service is the superior speed which it offers to the small, less than carload shipper.

It will be seen, therefore, that freight forwarding is essentially a volume business. Unless the freight forwarder can develop a large and regular volume of business, it cannot offer the expedited service which is the principle justification for its existence. It must obtain a sufficient volume to meet the carload minimum weight requirements of the railroads. It must obtain this volume day in and day out with regularity, for the objective of speed is defeated if the forwarder is required to hold freight on its platform for several days waiting to accumulate enough to make up a carload. It must obtain this large, regular volume at a reasonable number of points throughout the origin territory which it serves. For example, if a forwarder were to load cars only at Chicago, freight originating at Louisville, Kentucky and destined to New Orleans, Louisiana, would have to be trucked 300 miles to Chicago in the opposite direction from its ultimate destination. Its total journey would comprise 1250 miles, whereas the distance from Louisville to New Orleans is only 730 miles. Thus, again, the objective of speed in transit would have been defeated through the inability of the forwarder to load a car at or close to Louisville. The same thing is true in the destination territory sought to be served. If the forwarder does not have a sufficient volume of freight to enable it to consign cars to numerous points strategically located throughout its destination territory and is compelled to route all shipments through one break-bulk point, then many shipments must undergo a long, time consuming, off-line truck haul before they reach their ultimate destination.

In other words, the entire forwarder method of operation is dependent upon the availability of a large and regular volume of business. With such a volume, the forwarder can perform a useful and economic transportation service. Without it, the service which can be offered has no advantage over the less than carload service of the underlying carriers.

This volume is achieved through the channelization of traffic. Where a dozen competing routes each obtain a small portion of the total available quantity of traffic, no individual portion may be sufficient to permit movement in a through car from origin to destination without intermediate rehandling. The forwarder concentrates the entire volume into one channel of movement. This permits the loading of through cars, avoids intermediate rehandling, and produces the faster service which attracts the forwarders' patronage. Thus, the freight forwarder performs a function which the underlying carriers cannot perform themselves. By freely employing any railroad or truck line which can best perform the transportation service required and by coordinating the use of the facilities of all available underlying carriers, the forwarder accomplishes a concentration and channelization of traffic which the individual carriers cannot accomplish. However, the total volume of traffic available for movement in forwarder service is approximately constant. The annual reports of the Interstate Commerce Commission show that there is relatively little fluctuation in forwarder traffic from year to year. It follows, therefore, that as more and more newcomers to the field obtain a portion of that traffic, each individual forwarder's share of the total volume will be less and as a result their ability to concentrate the volume needed for efficient operation will be correspondingly diminished. That this is not an imaginary fear is demonstrated by the fact that in 1938 the Commission found that there were some twenty freight forwarders engaged in business,[1] whereas at the present time the Commission has issued permits to approximately 100 applicants, to say nothing of the numerous applications which are still pending and the even more numerous unregulated "pool car consolidators" and "shippers associations" which have sprung up in recent years. An example of the latter is now before the Court on appeal from the District Court of the United States for the Southern District of California, Central Division, in *Pacific Coast Wholesalers Association v. U. S.*

Under the principles established by the Commission in its decision in this proceeding the flood gates are opened wide for any one to enter the field of freight forwarding. This result comes about not so much as a result of what the Commission said or did, but as a result of what it did not say and did not do. In other words, the Commission failed to enforce and apply the requirements of the statute. It failed to require the applicant to sustain the burden of proving that its proposed service meets the statutory tests which are prerequisite to the issuance of a permit; and it has ignored, or arbitrarily disregarded substantial evidence tending to show that this proposal would not meet those tests. If, through failure of the Commission to enforce the provisions of the statute, the freight forwarding field is to be left wide open to all who choose to enter, diffusion and dispersion of traffic and economic chaos is the inevitable result.

One cardinal principle of public utility regulation has always been that the utility regulated and the public which depends upon it shall be accorded protection against uneco-

---

[1] *Freight Forwarding Investigation*, 229 I.C.C. 201, 203.

nomic and destructive competition. The language chosen
by the Congress in drafting Part IV of the Interstate Commerce Act was clearly intended to extend this protection to
the regulated freight forwarding industry. Yet, the construction which the Commission has placed upon the statute
would nullify that protection and will encourage the very
destructive competition which it is the duty of the Commission to prevent. In the circumstances we respectfully
submit that this appeal presents not only a substantial
question, but one of urgent importance to the entire regulated forwarding industry and to the shipping public.

2. The Evidence and the Findings

The applicant for the freight forwarder permit which
is the subject matter of this proceeding, Lifschultz Fast
Freight, already is engaged in the performance of a freight
forwarder service between Boston, New York and Phila-
delphia on the one hand and the Chicago area on the other
hand. It has successfully conducted this operation for
many years and has adequate financial resources. By the
instant application it seeks authority to extend its service
to the west and southwest. It offered no evidence to show
that it can successfully conduct this extended operation;
that it can establish a sufficient number of stations to perform an adequate service; or what volume of traffic it has
any expectation of obtaining. Instead, it apparently rested
upon its past record of successful operation in the east as
creating a presumption of ability to operate with similar
success in the west and southwest. These plaintiffs offered
substantial evidence intended to rebut this presumption
if indeed such a presumption exists. This will be discussed below. Upon this state of the record the Commission found

> "Applicant's readiness and ability to perform the
> service is not questioned. The long experience of ap-

plicant and its predecessors and its financial condition, together with other evidence of record, establish that it is ready and able to perform the service for which authority is granted." (265 I. C. C. 431, 445)

Defendants rely upon the above quoted finding of the Commission to support the ultimate conclusion required by the statute "that the applicant is ready, able and willing properly to perform the service proposed."

The application was supported by fourteen shippers who now use applicant's present service and who stated that they would use the proposed service if it is instituted. Only one of these fourteen witnesses gave any indication of the approximate volume of his traffic or the points to or from which it would move. Only four of them definitely asserted that they have the right to control the routing of the freight which they ship. Seven of them unequivocally stated that they would not use the proposed service unless it was at least as fast as that provided by existing forwarders. Upon this state of the record the Commission found:

"The shippers supporting the application use applicant's service between Chicago and points in trunk line and New England territories. They have received more prompt pick-up service and earlier delivery from applicant than from other forwarders. In addition, its efficient tracing and claim adjustment services have contributed to their preference for applicant. They anticipate similar advantages through use of the extended service here proposed, and their support is prompted by this consideration.

Witnesses supporting the application are shipping between the points here involved by rail, truck, express and air, as well as by freight forwarders. Their desire for applicant's proposed service warrants the inference that they would ship some part of their traffic in that service. Upon cross examination, however, they state that the services of existing forwarders have been generally satisfactory." (265 I. C. C. 431, 433-434)

Defendants rely upon the above quoted finding of the Commission to support the ultimate conclusion required by the statute "that the proposed service, to the extent authorized by the permit, is or will be consistent with the public interest and the national transportation policy declared in this Act."

3. The Findings of the Commission Do Not Have Substantial Support in the Evidence and Do Not Provide a Rational Basis for the Conclusion Reached.

The statute provides two standards, both of which must be met before the Commission may authorize the issuance of a freight forwarder permit. The Commission is required to find that a proposed forwarder service will conform with these standards.

These provisions appear in Section 410 (c) of the Interstate Commerce Act (49 U. S. C. 1010(c)). The first standard is:

> "* * * that the applicant is ready, able and willing properly to perform the service proposed."

We respectfully submit that the Commission's conclusion with reference to this requirement has no substantial support in the evidence and provides no rational basis for the Commission's ultimate decision. The District Court did not discuss this issue but merely affirmed the Commission's decision without opinion.

The significance of this requirement is greater than might appear upon the surface. Offhand, the public interest might not seem to be affected one way or another if this applicant is permitted to attempt to perform the proposed forwarder service, the only obvious consequence of its

failure being its personal loss of money expended in the
attempt. However, we direct the Court's attention to the
language of the statute. The applicant must not merely
prove that it is "able" to perform some sort of mediocre
service. It is specifically required to prove that it will
be *able to perform the service proposed.* Of the fourteen
witnesses who supported the application, seven stated that
they would not use the proposed service unless it was at
least as fast as that of existing forwarders. Nor can it
be inferred that the remaining seven have different views
since not all were asked this question, and since, as previously shown, speed in transit is the one feature, above all
others, which attracts patronage to the freight forwarder.
Therefore, unless this applicant is physically able to perform a service which is comparable with that of other forwarders, it could not expect to attract patronage and the
testimony of the shippers upon which the Commission's
report relies so heavily is nullified.

The evidence offered by these plaintiffs, which was completely ignored by the Commission, shows that many forwarders now operating in the territory involved in this
application, are unable to obtain a sufficient volume of
traffic to provide an adequate service throughout this broad
territory. Their annual reports filed with the Interstate
Commerce Commission show that many of these forwarders
have barely enough tonnage to exist—far too little to provide an adequate or comprehensive service. Within recent
years two freight forwarders have gone bankrupt attempting to operate into the State of Texas.

Applicant's evidence fails to disclose wherein its proposed venture would meet with any greater success. Applicant's testimony was that it *hopes* to operate by joint
loading with other freight forwarders. Joint loading con-
sists of two or more freight forwarders combining their
tonnage in order to make up the required carload minimum

weight. However, *applicant has no contract with any other freight forwarder who is willing to joint load with it and no prospect of obtaining such a contract.*

Applicant stated that it would make full use of the privilege of stopping cars off in transit for partial unloading which is permitted under applicable rail tariffs. However, only one stop in transit is permitted in the southwest. Thus, to give adequate service to the State of Texas alone, even though it could serve two destinations with one car, applicant would have to establish break-bulk stations in numerous different cities throughout the State. It disclosed no specific plans for the establishment of such stations nor does the record show that it has any prospect of obtaining the volume of tonnage necessary to make regular cars to this number of stations.

To the west coast the railroad rate structure is such that miscellaneous commodities cannot be freely mixed in a single car. This means that to avoid prohibitive penalties, applicant must forward a minimum of two cars at one time. Where this applicant will obtain the necessary tonnage to overcome this problem is not disclosed upon the record.

Unless this applicant can overcome these problems it will not be able to perform a service which will attract the patronage of the shipping public in general nor even the patronage of the fourteen shippers who supported the application. The mere fact that applicant has operated successfully in the east where traffic density is high and distances are relatively less than in the west and southwest affords no reasonable basis for presuming that in establishing a new operation in a new and different territory, the applicant is automatically assured of success. Thus, wholly apart from the question of whether this applicant is to be permitted to dissipate its financial resources, there remains the important question of whether it will be able to perform the service which it proposes and upon which the shipper support which it obtained was predicated.

As stated, the Commission ignored the voluminous and substantial evidence offered by these plaintiffs tending to show that applicant would not be able to perform such a service. Moreover, the Commission is guilty of a misstatement in holding that applicant's readiness and ability to perform the service is not questioned. Its readiness and ability was vigorously questioned at all times by these plaintiffs. The Commission's finding that applicant's long experience and adequate financial resources establish that it is ready and able to perform the service for which authority is granted is wholly unresponsive to the issue, is unsupported by any evidence bearing directly upon the proposed new service, and is contrary to the only evidence of record which is addressed specifically to this issue. The issue is not whether this applicant could operate successfully in the east. The issue is whether it can successfully conduct a new operation in a new and different territory. With reference to that proposed new operation, it stands in the same position as any newcomer and the record is wholly devoid of any evidence tending to show that it can successfully perform the operation it proposes.

The second standard imposed by Section 410 (c) of the Interstate Commerce Act is:

> "* * * that the proposed service, to the extent authorized by the permit, is or will be consistent with the public interest and the national transportation policy declared in this Act."

This same language has appeared elsewhere in the Act since 1935. In that year it was enacted in Section 209 (b) of the Motor Carrier Act (49 U. S. C. 309(b)). Subsequently, it was used in Section 309 (g), Part III of the Interstate Commerce Act, which regulates water carriers,

(49 U. S. C. 909 (g)). Therefore, when the Congress again used this same language in enacting Part III of the Interstate Commerce Act in 1942 it is to be presumed that it was intended to have the same meaning which had been previously attributed to it.[2]

The meaning of the phrase "public interest" was defined by the Supreme Court in *New York Central Securities Corporation* v. *U. S.*, 287 U. S. 12, 23, as follows:

> "* *- *' The term 'public interest' thus used is not a concept without ascertainable criteria but has direct relation to adequacy of transportation service, to its essential conditions of economy and efficiency, and to appropriate provision and best use of transportation facilities * * *."

Subsequently, after the addition of the national transportation policy to the Act, the Supreme Court in *McLean Trucking Company* v. *U. S.*, 321 U. S. 67, 82, cited the *New York Central Securities* case with approval and went further by characterizing the national transportation policy as "the Commission's guide to the public interest."

Construing the corresponding provisions of Section 209 (b) of the Motor Carrier Act, the Interstate Commerce Commission held

> "The term 'consistent with the public interest' means not against or contradictory to the public interest and must be considered in connection with the national transportation policy of Congress which places emphasis on the maintenance of safe, adequate, economic and efficient service, sound economic conditions in transportation and the preservation of a national transportation system adequate to meet the needs of commerce." *Worm Extension—Ainsworth and Johnstown, Nebraska*, 32 M. C. C. 641, 644.

[2] *U. S.* v. *Missouri Pacific Railroad Company*, 278 U. S. 269; *Great Northern Railroad Company* v. *U. S.*, 315 U. S. 262; *Fonderen* v. *Commissioner of Internal Revenue*, 324 U. S. 18.

Not only is the national transportation policy expressly incorporated in Section 410 (c) of the Act, with which we are here concerned, but that policy itself provides that all of the provisions of the Act shall be administered and enforced with a view to carrying out this declaration of policy.

From the foregoing it is abundantly clear that the standard of consistency with the public interest and the national transportation policy, as set forth in Section 410 (c) of the Act, contemplates the provision and maintenance of adequate, economical and efficient transportation service within the freight forwarding field. To support a conclusion that this standard has been complied with, the Commission's order should contain some finding or findings which in substance declare that these objectives have been met. The report from which this appeal is taken contains no such findings nor does the record before the Commission contain any evidence upon which such findings could be based.

There is no evidence that the proposed service will be intrinsically adequate, economical or efficient and there is substantial evidence tending to show that it will not. This has been covered in our discussion of applicant's "ability" to perform the service which it proposes. As shown, this applicant intends to inaugurate a new service in a new territory under new operating conditions. The evidence shows that there are many substantial problems to be overcome before such service can be successfully performed. The record contains not one iota of evidence to show that this applicant can successfully meet these problems and neither the Commission nor the Court made any findings addressed to this issue.

The single affirmative finding which the Commission made, which is relied upon by defendants, was that fourteen shippers will probably patronize the new service to some unspecified extent. In the first place, seven of these shippers stated that they would not patronize the proposed service unless it is at least as fast as that of other forwarders. Thus, in the absence of any showing by applicant that its proposed service will equal the service of other forwarders, it cannot be assumed that it will attract the patronage of even the few shippers who appeared in support of the application. Of greater importance, however, is the fact that testimony of this type is not responsive to the issue. The issue is whether this proposed service will be conducive to the maintenance of adequate, economic and efficient forwarder service. Even if it be assumed that all fourteen of these shippers would patronize this new service extensively, that fact is only remotely relevant and is certainly not persuasive that the proposed service will be consistent with the standards of adequacy, economy and efficiency imposed by the statute.

As stated by the Commission in *Jamestown, N. Y., C. of C. v. Jamestown, W. & N. W. R. Co.*, 195 I. C. C. 289, 292:

> "The expression 'in the public interest' means more than a mere desire on the part of shippers or other interested parties for something that would be convenient or desirable to them. Where something substantial is to be taken away from a carrier for the sole benefit of such parties, and with no corresponding benefit to the carrier, as in this case, we are inclined to the view that some actual necessity or some compelling reason must first be shown before we can find such action in the public interest. In determining what is 'in the public interest' we must take into consideration not only the interests of the particular shippers at or near the terminal considered, but also the interests of the carriers and of the general public."

If this applicant cannot establish the necessary facilities and if it cannot generate the necessary tonnage to provide an adequate or efficient service, the mere fact that it obtains some patronage does not cure this deficiency. If this proposed new service impairs existing forwarders' service to the detriment of the public and in contravention of the national transportation policy, that result is none the less inconsistent with the provisions of the Act simply because the applicant is able to attract some business. Therefore, the questions which are implicit in the practical application of the standards of adequacy, economy and efficiency are not answered by the fact that a few shippers may patronize the proposed service, but demand more specific and unequivocal proof. No such proof appears in the record before the Commission.

Apart from the lack of proof or of findings that the proposed service will itself be adequate and efficient, there remains the question of whether, by diverting traffic from existing forwarders, it may impair the over-all forwarder service which the public is now receiving. This is the only major issue presented by this case which was considered in detail by the Commission. Even with respect to this issue, however, the Commission's conclusions have no substantial support in the evidence.

Section 410 (d) of the Interstate Commerce Act modifies Section 410 (c) to a limited extent. It provides in substance that no application for a freight forwarder permit shall be denied *solely* because the proposed service will be competitive with the service of existing forwarders. By this provision it is evident that the Congress intended that no application should be denied simply because adequate forwarder service already existed in the territory proposed to be served.

The word "solely" which appears in this Section of the Act is of special significance for two reasons.

First, it makes clear that Congress did not intend to preclude consideration of the competitive effect of a proposed new service, but merely intended that adequacy of existing services, standing alone, should not be a sufficient ground to deny a permit. The Commission itself has twice recognized that this interpretation of the statute is correct. In *Schneider Brothers and Company, Inc. Freight Forwarder Application,* FF 176, mimeographed, decided November 13, 1947, it declined to issue a freight forwarder permit where the effect of the proposed new service, transcending mere healthy competition, would have been to materially impair the sum total of existing forwarder service to the public. Likewise, in its report in the instant proceeding, the Commission stated:

> "We do not mean to say that Section 410 (d) precludes denial of an application where it is shown that a proposed service would result in impairment of forwarder service in general within the affected territory. If a substantial impairment is threatened or reasonably to be anticipated in the event such new service is instituted, that result clearly would be contrary to the public interest and the national transportation policy." (265 I. C. C. 431, 444)

From the foregoing it is clear that Section 410 (d), (1) does not preclude the Commission from considering the competitive effect of a proposed service or from basing the denial of an application partly upon such competitive effect, if other factors in addition to competition also enter into its conclusion and (2) does not preclude denying an application when the granting thereof would result in such destructive competition as to be inconsistent with the public interest and the national transportation policy, which overrides all other provisions of the Act.

In the circumstances we respectfully submit that nothing contained in Section 410 (d) would preclude denial of this application. As shown above, the applicant has failed to prove that it will be able to perform the service that it proposes or that such service will conform with the standards of adequacy, economy and efficiency imposed by Section 410 (c) and by the national transportation policy. Therefore, wholly apart from the competitive effect of the proposed service, the inadequacy of applicant's proof, alone, warrants denial of the application. This being so, the Commission is not prohibited from also taking into consideration the competitive effect of the proposed service if, in its judgment, this is a proper element to be considered.

If the Commission had found that the proposed new service would be destructive in its competitive effect, contrary to the public interest and the national transportation policy, Section 410 (d) would not preclude denial of the application. It is true that as to this issue the Commission found to the contrary but its finding amounts to a denial of due process. First, the Commission excused the applicant from describing in specific detail what service it proposed to render and what points it proposed to serve. While it may not be incumbent upon the Commission to require the applicant to adduce such evidence, it is incumbent upon the Commission to deny an application when such evidence is lacking. Had this applicant stated specifically that it proposed to serve, for example, Odessa, Texas, these plaintiffs could have demonstrated with mathematical certainty, either that the applicant could not serve Odessa or the alternative, that if it succeeded existing service would be impaired. Likewise, had applicant disclosed that it proposed to serve Odessa, Texas by some indirect or inefficient means, plaintiffs could have shown that its service would be inferior and that even the shippers that supported the application would not patronize such a service.

As the record stands, since the applicant did not disclose with particularity what it proposes to do, plaintiffs necessarily were unable to show with particularity where or the extent to which their service would be injured. Their testimony and evidence was necessarily general. The Commission concluded that such testimony and evidence failed to prove that the proposed service would be destructive in its competitive effect. Thus, by failing to enforce the proper standards of proof with respect to this applicant, the Commission precluded plaintiffs from demonstrating the true extent to which this proposal threatens to impair existing forwarder service. To hold that Section 410 (d) requires this result, is to hold that it supersedes Section 410 (c) and the national transportation policy.

The second significance of the word "solely" in Section 410 (d) is that it has an important bearing upon the legislative history of the Act. Representative Wolverton, who was a minority member of the House Committee on Interstate and Foreign Commerce and who was active in connection with the passage of this legislation, made two lengthy statements upon the floor of the House purporting to explain the meaning of the bill and the reason for the Committee's recommendations. Certain statements made by Representative Wolverton are quoted by the Commission in its report herein in support of its construction of the statute to the effect that freight forwarder permits should be issued liberally. Since, as shown, Section 410 (c) is a counterpart of similar provisions in other Parts of the Act, which provisions have been uniformly construed for many years, the only justification for resort to legislative history lies in Section 410 (d) which is new to the Interstate Commerce Act. If greater liberality was intended under Part IV than under the similar provisions of Parts II and III, and if we are to be regulated by the statute, rather than by speeches made on the floor of the House, the basis for such greater liberality must be found in Section 410 (d).

Representative Wolverton had introduced a bill of his own, H. R. 5179, 77th Congress, First Session, in which the substantive provisions of Section 410 (d) appeared for the first time. This bill was considered by the Committee along with the prior bill, S. 210, which was already before it. The Committee as a whole adopted the proposed new section but added the word "solely". With respect to this particular provision, therefore, the Committee as a whole expressed and manifested its disagreement with Representative Wolverton.

Not only does this act by the Committee clearly indicate that its views were not the same as Representative Wolverton's, but it is also significant to note that the Committee Report, House Report No. 1172, 77th Congress, First Session, had been circulated for approximately nine months before the bill was finally passed. No member of the Committee, including Representative Wolverton, demanded a recall of the report or filed a minority report.

Furthermore, a fair construction of Representative Wolverton's remarks does not support the interpretation which the Commission has placed upon them. His comments with reference to the permit section of the Act merely purport to explain why the Committee had chosen the standard of "consistency with the public interest and the national transportation policy" rather than the standard of "public convenience and necessity" which was originally contained in the Senate version of the bill. Admittedly, the standard adopted is a more liberal one than the standard of "public convenience and necessity." However, as previously shown, it has a well established meaning and nothing contained in Representative Wolverton's remarks justifies the inference that a departure from that meaning was intended. In passing, it might be noted that Representative Wolverton's major premise was that "the primary purpose of requiring a certificate as a prerequisite to operate is to protect the public from having to support improvident investments in transportation facilities.'' This statement was cited by the Commission at page 441 of its report. Plausible as it may sound, it is not true. Countless decisions of the Commission affirm the fact that protection of the public from irresponsible or improvident operation and from effects of destructive competition between carriers are at least equally important reasons for the imposition of the several certificate and permit requirements contained in the Act.[3]

The construction of the Act which the Commission has derived through consideration of Representative Wolverton's remarks, goes far beyond the reasonable intent of the statute. Although the Commission contents itself with stating that in its opinion freight forwarder permits are to be issued more liberally than motor carrier permits, in practical effect its construction of the statute ignores all of the affirmative requirements imposed thereby.

As we have shown, the language of Section 410 (c) is substantially the same as the language of corresponding provisions in Parts II and III of the Act. The only difference is that created by Section 410 (d) which imposes the qualification that no application should be denied *solely* on the ground that the proposed service will compete with existing service. Therefore, the same principles of law and the same standards of proof should be invoked under Part IV as were invoked under Parts II and III except to the limited extent that a difference is specifically required by. Section 410 (d). Yet, pursuant to its desire to be liberal

---

[3] *Motor Bus and Motor Truck Operation*, 140 I.C.C. 685, 737; *Coordination of Motor Transportation*, 182 I.C.C. 263, 371; *C & D Oil Company, Contract Carrier Application*, I M.C.C. 329; *Worm Extension, Ainsworth and Johnstown, Nebraska*, 32 M.C.C. 641, 644; *Welsh Contract Carrier Application*, 8 M.C.C. 687; *Woods Contract Carrier Application*, 7 M.C.C. 193; *William Heim Cartage Co.-Extension, Indianapolis*, 20 M.C.C. 329.

in the issuance of forwarder permits, the Commission has failed to require of this applicant any proof whatsoever that it will be able to perform the new service which is the subject matter of the application. *Section 410 (d) does not call for this construction of the Act either expressly or by implication.*

The Commission has in effect ignored extensive and substantial evidence offered by these plaintiffs tending to show that this applicant will not be able to conduct the service which it proposes; that such service will not be adequate, efficient and economic; and that such service will seriously threaten to impair existing forwarder service to the public. *Such arbitrary and capricious rejection of substantial evidence is not required, either expressly or by implication, by Section 410 (d).*

This point is nowhere better illustrated than in the Commission's own language taken from its report. It found at page 439 of its report that such traffic as this applicant might obtain would, for the most part, be diverted from other forwarders and, at page 442, that upon this record it could not form any reliable estimate as to the probable extent of such diversion. Then it concluded at page 444 that no substantial impairment was threatened or reasonably to be anticipated as a result of this proposed new service.

If the Commission could not estimate the probable extent to which this new service would take business from existing forwarders, (and it could not, for the record is wholly inadequate), how could it conclude, as a fact, that existing forwarder service would not be substantially injured?

By the same token, since the applicant did not describe how it proposed to succeed in an operation where many others have failed, upon what "substantial" evidence did the Commission find that this applicant would be "able" to perform the service proposed?

In the circumstances, we respectfully submit that this appeal presents a substantial question affecting the welfare of the forwarding industry as a whole and of the public which depends upon freight forwarder service. We assert that the Commission has gravely erred in its interpretation of the statute and as a result of such error, has arbitrarily and capriciously ignored substantial evidence and that its findings and conclusions have no substantial support in the evidence nor do they provide a rational basis for its ultimate conclusion that this application should be granted. Whereas, we respectfully pray that the motion of defendants-appellees be denied.

Respectfully submitted,

DAVID AXELROD,
39 South La Salle Street,
Chicago 3, Illinois;
JAMES L. GIVAN,
1346 Connecticut Avenue, N. W.,
Washington 6, D. C.,
Attorneys for Plaintiffs-Appellants.

Of Counsel:

TURNEY, CARPENTER & TURNEY,
1346 Connecticut Avenue,
Washington 6, D. C.

Due Date: August 31, 1949.

IN THE DISTRICT COURT OF THE UNITED STATES FOR THE NORTHERN DISTRICT OF ILLINOIS, EASTERN DIVISION

Civil No. 49 C 409

ACME FAST FREIGHT, INC., ET AL.,

Plaintiffs-Appellants,

vs.

UNITED STATES OF AMERICA AND INTERSTATE COMMERCE COMMISSION,

Defendants-Appellees

SUPPLEMENT TO PLAINTIFFS-APPELLANTS' REPLY TO DEFENDANTS-APPELLEES' MOTION TO AFFIRM.

Plaintiffs-appellants respectfully request that their Reply to Defendants-Appellees' Motion to Affirm be supplemented to include reference to the following decision of the United States Court of Appeals for the District of Columbia. This decision is pertinent to the question of the sufficiency of proof of applicant's fitness, willingness and ability and should be considered in conjunction with the argument which appears on pages 7, 8 and 9 of the reply which is hereby supplemented. Reference to this decision was inadvertently omitted from such reply.

The decision referred to is *State Airlines, Inc. v. Civil Aeronautics Board, et al.,* 174 F. 2d 510, decided by the

United States Court of Appeals for the District of Columbia on April 6, 1949 and now pending before the Supreme Court on petitions for Writs of Certiorari. This case arose out of a decision by the Civil Aeronautics Board in which the Board awarded a certificate of public convenience and necessity to Piedmont Aviation, Inc. Piedmont had applied for certain routes and had adduced evidence tending to prove that the service proposed was required by the public convenience and necessity and that it was fit, willing, and able properly to perform such service. The routes applied for by Piedmont were north-south routes lying east of the Appalachian Mountains. The Board granted Piedmont an extensive network of routes far in excess of those applied for including many routes which crossed the Appalachians. One issue before the Court was whether the Board's order was supported by sufficient evidence of Piedmont's fitness, willingness and ability to operate the routes granted. With reference to this issue the Court held:

"However, the Board also found, using the precise terminology of the Act, that Piedmont was fit, willing and able to perform properly the air transportation found required, and to comply with the rules, regulations and requirements of the Board. It is this latter finding which is not only unjustified on the basis of the record, but unjustifiable. In Braniff Airways, Inc. v. Civil Aeronautics Board, this court said:

'The Act does not define ''fit, willing and able'' but the Board has established these tests: (1) a proper organizational basis for the conduct of air transportation; (2) a plan for the conduct of the service made by competent personnel; (3) adequate financial resources.'

That opinion went on to state that a finding by the Board, when made, was supported by substantial evidence of the fitness, willingness, and ability of the applicant in that case, but this court then reversed the Board because there was evidence of changed conditions since the Board made that finding which required a new hearing so that present facts could be determined. In the instant case, we have presented the still stronger situation wherein, even at the time of the Board's finding that Piedmont was fit, willing, and able, there was *no* evidence of Piedmont's appropriate qualification for the awarded routes. We find the record before us barren of any evidence put in by Piedmont to show its fitness, willingness, or ability to operate west of the Appalachians or over mountainous terrain.'' (Pages 516-517)

''It does not follow, and we believe it cannot follow, that proof of fitness, willingness, and ability to operate along basically north-south routes, paralleling existent surface travel, and avoiding mountainous terrain is equivalent to proof of qualification to operate on basically east-west routes, generally at right angles to the major lines of flow of existing surface travel, and crossing large areas of a very mountainous region. The absurdity of such a claim is demonstrated by the extreme position which counsel for the Board was compelled to take in oral argument before this court in defense of the action taken by the Board. When questioned from the bench in oral argument before us, counsel for respondent Board admitted that it was the Board's claim that if Piedmont had applied for a route from Hagerstown to Norfolk in a southeastern area proceeding, the Board could award Piedmont the Miami to Jacksonville route. In such a case, as in the case at issue, the sociological, economic and topographical factors are so variable as to render any attempt to use such factors as are introduced to support the granting of a particular route totally valueless in considering another and substantially different route.'' (Page 518)

We respectfully submit that the above cited case is on all fours with the issue presented by this appeal. In the *Piedmont* case, Piedmont presented evidence tending to show that it was fit, willing and able to operate east of the

Appalachian Mountains. In the *Lifschultz* case the applicant presented evidence tending to show that it is fit, willing and able to operate between the Atlantic Seaboard and Chicago.

In the *Piedmont* case the Court held that proof of ability to operate east of the Appalachian Mountains would not support a finding by the Civil Aeronautics Board that Piedmont was able to operate across the mountains. We urge the Court to reach a similar conclusion in the instant proceeding. As we have already argued at length, the mere fact that this applicant has been able to operate successfully in the east does not support a finding that its proposed operation will meet with equal success in a new area where, in the language of the Court, "the sociological, economic and topographical factors are so variable as to render any attempt to use such factors as are introduced to support the granting of a particular route totally valueless in considering another and substantially different route."

Respectfully submitted,

DAVID AXELROD,
39 South La Salle Street,
Chicago 3, Illinois;
JAMES L. GIVAN,
1346 Connecticut Avenue, N. W.,
Washington 6, D. C.,
Attorneys for Plaintiffs-Appellants.

Of Counsel:

TURNEY, CARPENTER & TURNEY,
1346 Connecticut Avenue, N. W.,
Washington 6, D. C.

Dated: September 1, 1949.

(4309)

CPSIA information can be obtained
at www.ICGtesting.com
Printed in the USA
LVOW09s1412230517
535500LV00024BA/546/P